I'M
STILL
WRITING

I'M STILL WRITING

WOMEN WRITERS ON CREATIVITY, COURAGE, AND PUTTING WORDS ON THE PAGE

Virginia Ann Byrd

ST. MARTIN'S
ESSENTIALS
NEW YORK

First published in the United States by St. Martin's Essentials,
an imprint of St. Martin's Publishing Group

I'M STILL WRITING. Copyright © 2023 by St. Martin's Essentials.
All rights reserved. Printed in the United States of America.
For information, address St. Martin's Publishing Group,
120 Broadway, New York, NY 10271.

www.stmartins.com

Library of Congress Cataloging-in-Publication Data

Names: Byrd, Virginia Ann, author.
Title: I'm still writing : women writers on creativity, courage, and
   putting words on the page / Virginia Ann Byrd.
Description: First edition. | New York : St. Martin's Essentials, 2023. |
   Includes bibliographical references.
Identifiers: LCCN 2022045389 | ISBN 9781250875037 (trade paperback) |
   ISBN 9781250875044 (ebook)
Subjects: LCSH: Authorship—Quotations, maxims, etc. | Authors—Quotations. |
   Women—Authorship. | Creative writing—Problems, exercises, etc. |
   Authorship—Problems, exercises, etc.
Classification: LCC PN165 .B97 2023 | DDC 808.02082—dc23/eng/20221025
LC record available at https://lccn.loc.gov/2022045389

Our books may be purchased in bulk for promotional, educational, or business use. Please
contact your local bookseller or the Macmillan Corporate and
Premium Sales Department at 1-800-221-7945, extension 5442, or
by email at MacmillanSpecialMarkets@macmillan.com.

First Edition: 2023

10 9 8 7 6 5 4 3 2 1

Contents

CONTENTS

CONTENTS

Introduction

Welcome to *I'm Still Writing*!

This book is designed to spark your creativity and help you build a thriving creative practice by sharing the words and wisdom of female writers. It is divided into fifty-two chapters, one for each week of the year. Each chapter includes a passage from a brilliant writer on the art and craft of writing. You'll find that some of them are incredibly practical and some of them are more conceptual, but all offer useful insights and food for thought. In addition to a quotation, each week has two sections that invite you to engage with the writer of the week: Listen and Write. The Listen sections include questions to help you reflect and dig a little deeper into the material you just read. Reading about writing and thinking about writing are all well and good, but it also generally helps to actually *do* it as well. That's where the Write sections come into play. Each features a writing exercise inspired by the ideas you've read and explored that week.

Meet the Writers

The authors collected in this book are some of the best known and most beloved female writers who have ever put pen to paper. These authors and their work are the instructors behind *I'm Still Writing*, patron saints of the artistic variety. They are women who have done and are continuing to do the work of writing with strength and intelligence.

The list of writers who fit that description or who could have been included in this book is endless—there is so much to learn about this maddening, joyful craft and so many wise, adventurous women who can teach us. The writers featured in this book have been selected because they represent not only various time periods, perspectives, and styles of writing, but also different ways of thinking about creativity and the process of writing.

The passages in *I'm Still Writing* are from many different sources and contexts—from essays and interviews, lectures and personal letters. If one in particular resonates with you, you can find the exact source material listed in the Bibliography at the back of the book.

Some of the writers in these pages are dreaming up fantasy worlds and sci-fi creations, while others are crafting literary fiction and poetry. In *I'm Still Writing*, there's no hierarchy of importance around the genre of work you create.

As you read and write your way through this book, you will notice that many of these writers think about their work and craft very differently, sometimes even contradictorily. And what a relief that is! As it turns out, there is no one way to write a book or poem or essay. You have full permission to cheerfully ignore any piece of advice that doesn't work for you, no matter how illustrious the writer who first shared it. Listen to everything with openness and curiosity, but take only what suits you and your work.

How to Use This Book

You can proceed in neat numerical fashion through the book, one exercise a week for the whole year. That's the way the book is structured, and you'll have a grand time working through it that way! However, this is your book now and you can use it however you want. You might find it helpful to begin with chapters that focus on a theme or topic you need help with. For instance, if you're seriously stuck on dialogue, you could scoot right over to chapter 31 and let Anne Lamott tutor you. You may find that a weekly format is too ambitious or not ambitious enough—don't hesitate to adjust the pace to suit your own needs. Or you may want to skip right ahead to your favorite authors just because. Make the book work for you, whatever that looks like.

A Word on Time

Sometimes our ambitions can get just a little bit ahead of the reality of our lives. We envision reams of pages written and a stack of notebooks filled with ink-rippled pages. And then ... life sets in and we suddenly find ourselves choosing between taking a shower and having time to do laundry. That's why the exercises and questions in this book are brief—they're accessible and doable even if you only really have half an hour to spare before the insistent siren song of your work email or the wail of your toddler demands your attention.

There's something to be said for the encouragement we can find in accomplishing a creative exercise, however small. It builds our confidence and shows us that we *can* reach our goals and meet our own ambitions. The prompts in this book are a great way to do exactly that.

The weekly exercises in *I'm Still Writing* are also brief because they aren't necessarily meant to be the only writing in your life. Learning and developing your craft and technique is important, but it can never replace the need to do the actual work of writing your novel/screenplay/poem/memoir/essay.

These are lessons and creative springboards to help you learn and grow as you tackle the writing work you are burning to do.

Now, if you're in a season of life where you have the bandwidth to complete exactly one writing exercise a week and not a semicolon more, fear not! That is good, worthy creative work and you are learning and growing just fine. Creativity doesn't have an expiration date.

Regardless of where you are or what your creative ambition may be, the writers in these pages can inspire, challenge, and guide you. So grab a pen and paper (or, let's be honest, a laptop), brew yourself a cup of tea, and get writing!

—*Virginia Ann Byrd*

1

Toni Morrison

· MEMORY ·

" My job becomes how to rip that veil drawn over 'proceedings too terrible to relate.' The exercise is also critical for any person who is Black, or who belongs to any marginalized category, for historically, we were seldom invited to participate in the discourse even when we were its topic.

. . .

The act of imagination is bound up with memory. You know, they straightened out the Mississippi River in places, to make room for houses and livable acreage. Occasionally the river floods these places. 'Floods' is the word they use, but in fact it is not flooding; it is remembering. . . . Writers are like that: remembering where we were, what valley we ran through, what the banks were like, the light that was there, and the route back to our original place. . . . A rush of imagination is our 'flooding.' "

—"The Site of Memory"

LISTEN

What is your "original place"—that thing that repeats itself unavoidably in your memory? Perhaps it's a physical location, an emotion, a fragment of a memory, a relationship. Memory is often the foundation of imagination, so it's worth exploring.

The memories Morrison references here are ones that have been silenced and hidden, but Morrison considers it her work to "rip" away the veil with her voice and her writing. Are there parts of your experience that have been marginalized or silenced in some way? Is there a veil you are burning to rip down?

WRITE

Write about a sensory memory, something you physically experienced that has lingered with you over time. It could be the feel of a muddy path beneath your feet, the bitter taste of old coffee in a dorm room at 2 AM, the stomach-plummeting moment when you lost your footing. Anything you remember viscerally and physically.

Begin by writing out the details of this memory as you recall it, but don't limit yourself to precise particulars of the factual moment. Allow your writing to expand and explore what feels natural—follow the threads between memory and imagination and see where they lead you.

2

Ursula K. Le Guin

· IMAGINATION AND EXPERIENCE ·

❝ Fiction results from imagination working on experience. We shape experience in our minds so that it makes sense. We force the world to be coherent, to tell us a story.

. . .

Experience is where ideas come from. But a story isn't a mirror of what happened. Fiction is experience translated by, transformed by, transfigured by the imagination. Truth includes but is not coextensive with fact. Truth in art is not imitation, but reincarnation.

To be valuable in a factual history, the raw material of experience has to be selected, arranged, and shaped. In a novel, the process is even more radical: the raw materials are not only selected and shaped but also fused, composted, recombined, reworked, reconfigured, reborn, and at the same time allowed to find their own forms and shapes, which may be only indirectly related to rational thinking—so that the whole thing may seem to be pure invention. . . . But there's no such thing as pure invention. Invention is recombination. We work only with what we have. It all starts with experience. There are monsters and leviathans and chimeras in the human mind; they are psychic facts. Dragons are one of the truths about us. **99**

—"Where Do You Get Your Ideas From?"

LISTEN

Le Guin beautifully connects the seemingly disparate concepts of imagination, experience, and invention. How do you understand the connection between these things in your own work?

Later in this essay, Le Guin notes that the lives of many great novelists (the Brontës or Austen, for instance) were quiet and seemingly unremarkable, with none of the wild experiences we might think would provide fodder for riveting novels. What do you think the "raw material of experience" consists of? What kind of experience creates powerful writers?

WRITE

Consider one of your favorite fairy tales, myths, or legends. Any story will do as long as it has a fantastical element. Now unravel it; find or reimagine the basic human story that underlies the fantasy. What series of regular events—the change of seasons, a war, a fractured family—could have inspired the myth?

To use Le Guin's framework, the story you're reading is the invention and now you are seeking to understand how the imagination of the original author created it from their experience. Imagine the original writer of the tale: What factual events inspired their fantastic creation?

You'll find that taking the dragons *out* of a story requires every bit as much creativity and imagination as writing them in in the first place. If you prefer, you can also try this exercise in reverse and recast an ordinary experience through the lens of fantasy to create a legend all your own.

3

Margaret Atwood

· TRUTH ·

66 Do the research. Cross-check everything for accuracy. Make sure you've got the facts. . . . Just because a thing ought to be true—just because you mean well—just because it fits your ideology—just because it would be very convenient in the general scheme of things if it *were* true—doesn't mean it *is* true. You need to be prepared to back up your facts because if you say something that is not popular, you will surely be attacked. Or to quote George Orwell: 'If liberty means anything at all, it means the right to tell people what they do not want to hear.' And to quote him again: three words: Tell. The. Truth. 99

—"Tell. The. Truth."

LISTEN

Questions about writing the truth, whether that means representing diverse characters fully and accurately or exhaustively fact-checking works of nonfiction, have lately come to the forefront of conversation in the literary world. What pieces of writing immediately come to mind when you think of writers who ignore ideology in favor of truth?

What does it really mean to, as Atwood commands, tell the truth in your particular sphere of the writing world? What does that look like in practice?

WRITE

Assumption is the nemesis of research, and it's often our assumptions, the things we reflexively believe to be true without taking the time to examine them further, that lead our writing astray. Spend some time revisiting a piece of writing you've already created. As you read it, question every line asking yourself: Is that true? Is that verifiable? Be relentless in rooting out your own assumptions. Some things to consider:

Fiction:

SETTING: If this is a real place, are the location details correct? If the world is completely imagined, is the environment cohesive and logical within the boundaries of the fictional world? Is your world-building well thought out?

CHARACTER: Is the dialogue accurate to how these characters would truly speak? Have you fallen into stereotypes or vague characterization?

PLOT: Do the characters' actions and responses make sense within the context of the story? Are there moments when you've subordinated the story itself to a larger ideological point?

Nonfiction:

What have you accepted as unstated presuppositions in your writing? They might be ideological, cultural, political, etc. Are these presuppositions truly universally accepted or are they debatable? Acknowledge and establish the premises of your work clearly for your reader.

What is your own bias and perspective on this issue? Read through your work paying attention to the blind spots that are inherent to someone writing from your viewpoint.

Do you have verification for all of the facts you've included? Are your sources reliable?

4

Alice Walker

· EMOTION ·

" In my new college of the young I am often asked, 'What is the place of hate in writing?' After all we have been through in this country it is foolish and in any case useless to say hate has no place. Obviously, it has. But we must exercise our noblest impulses with our hate . . . I've found, in my own writing, that a little hatred, keenly directed, is a useful thing. Once spread about, however, it becomes a web in which I would sit caught and paralyzed. . . . The strength of the artist is his courage to look at every old thing with fresh eyes and his ability to re-create, as true to life as possible, that great middle ground of people between Medgar Evers's murderer, Byron de la Beckwith, and the fine old gentleman John Brown. "

—"The Unglamorous but Worthwhile Duties of
the Black Revolutionary Artist, Or of the Black Writer
Who Simply Works and Writes"

LISTEN

Here Alice Walker writes about the role of hate in writing, specifically in the context of Black writers and artists wrestling with injustice and racism. In what ways do you think hate, or other strong emotions, can be a "useful thing" in writing and art? On the flip side, how can it become a paralyzing force?

What do you think the "middle ground" of reality that Walker discusses here looks like in practice? Are there works of fiction or nonfiction that you think walk this line, neither ignoring hate nor allowing it to define the work altogether?

WRITE

Reflect on your own tendencies in your writing—do you often write from a place of anger or do you tend to avoid that type of emotional conflict in your approach?

This week, think of a topic that enrages you—it might be something small and seemingly petty ("Use your turn signal, people!") or something vast and seemingly unapproachable (injustice, poverty). Allow yourself to feel and embrace all the hatred and frustration you feel on the subject and write about it.

Step away from that piece of writing and come back to it

with a fresh perspective later in the week—did your emotion give you a keen, sharp eye or do you find you wrote a rambling tirade that didn't make a point?

Try writing a second version of this piece that aims at the "middle ground" Walker talks about—not dismissing legitimate anger or ignoring complex realities, but being courageous enough to look at the situation honestly without hiding behind the emotional bulwark of anger.

5

Celeste Ng

❝ I write based on the characters, and then I outline what I already wrote. As if somebody else wrote it and I'm just trying to analyze it and figure it out.

When I taught writing, I used to call this 'reverse outlining' for my students. For me, that's helpful because I can step back and figure out what I'm saying in a way that I can't when I'm writing. You know, writing is always that sort of balance of going with your intuition and your inspiration and letting that romp free.

Then at some point, you also have to bring in the critic: *Does this make sense? Does this character follow an arc? Does this story work together?* And that's my way of balancing it. I let the story run first, then I step back and let the inner critic come in and look at what I've got and see if it makes sense. Then I stick them back in a box and I let the other one out again. **❞**

—Interview with *Writer's Digest*

LISTEN

Ng describes two different states that she finds herself inhabiting as she writes—one where her inspiration and intuition are allowed to "romp free" and a second where she is taking on the role of the objective "inner critic." Do you resonate with those two descriptions? Which voice do you more often channel in your writing?

In Ng's work, she leads with her more intuitive and less structured writing voice and follows that up with a more critical eye. Have you found that your own process follows a similar pattern or do you like to create a more established framework before letting your creativity loose?

WRITE

Try Ng's method of reverse outlining for yourself. Though Ng uses this method in her novels, the same approach can be helpful for writing in many genres.

Consider part of a project you're already working on and outline it *after* the words are on the page. You might just make bullet points for the contents of each chapter, jot down the main points of each paragraph in an essay on sticky notes— whatever makes sense to track the meaning of your words over the course of the piece.

Once you've created an outline for your work, step back and think critically about it. How is structure serving the writing—is it logical and fluid? How does the emotional arc of the piece function? Are there points that seem contrived or needlessly complex that could be smoothed? Don't be afraid to rework, rethink, and reconsider the bones of what you've written.

6

Agatha Christie

· HUMILITY ·

66 Certainly, when you begin to write, you are usually in the throes of admiration for some writer, and, whether you will or no, you cannot help copying their style. Often it is not a style that suits you, and so you write badly. But as time goes on you are less influenced by admiration. You still admire certain writers, you may even wish you could write like them, but you know quite well that you can't. Presumably you have learnt literary humility. If I could write like Elizabeth Bowen, Muriel Spark, or Graham Greene, I should jump to high heaven with delight, but I know that I can't, and it would never occur to me to attempt to copy them. I have learnt that I am *me,* that I can do the things that, as one might put it, *me* can do, but I cannot do the things that *me* would like to do. As the Bible says, 'Who by taking thought can add one cubit to his stature?' 99

—*Agatha Christie: An Autobiography*

LISTEN

Christie suggests that every writer begins with imitation. Have you found that to be true? Are there particular voices and styles of writing that you would "jump to high heaven" if you could emulate?

What do you think Christie intends with the phrase "literary humility"?

WRITE

Inspired by Christie's observations, take some time to evaluate your own strengths and style. Write a brief profile of your writing style: Is your diction lush and lyrical or precise and spare? Do you focus on dialogue, on character, on setting? What style and structure of sentences do you write best? Do you prefer emotive writing or intellectual writing? We're often more comfortable identifying our weaknesses instead of our strengths, particularly when it comes to writing, but part of getting to know your own voice is identifying both the areas where you can grow *and* the areas where you already shine.

Now, take a look at some material you've written recently and perform the same analysis. Is what you see on the page similar to how you characterized your writing style mentally?

What are the strongest parts of your writing? What are the areas that need continued development? By getting to know the "me" of your own voice, you'll be better able to find your style and hone your writing.

7

Zadie Smith

· EDITING ·

66 [This] is the only absolutely twenty-four-karat-gold-plated piece of advice I have to give you. I've never taken it myself, though one day I hope to. The advice is as follows.

When you finish your novel, if money is not a desperate priority, if you do not need to sell it at once or be published that very second—*put it in a drawer.* For as long as you can manage. A year or more is ideal—but even three months will do. *Step away from the vehicle.* The secret to editing your work is simple: you need to become its reader instead of its writer.

· · ·

You need a certain head on your shoulders to edit a novel, and it's not the head of a writer in the thick of it, nor the head of a professional editor who's read it in twelve different versions. It's the head of a smart stranger who picks it off a bookshelf and begins to read. 99

—**"That Crafty Feeling"**

LISTEN

Smith says that the secret to editing your work is "to become its reader instead of its writer." How does a reader approach a text in a way that is fundamentally different from a writer?

What qualities does "a smart stranger" bring as a reader? How can you channel more of those qualities when you approach the work of others?

WRITE

If you have a well-aged writing project that you've tucked away in a folder somewhere, perfect! Take this invitation to dip back into it. If you don't have a desk-drawer project to edit, develop your editorial skills by trying this same exercise with a chapter or essay from another writer.

As you read, focus on approaching the work receptively, as a reader, instead of proactively, as a writer. Cast yourself in the role of the smart stranger and try to approach the writing from a distance, but with the same attention and interest you would give to a good book-club book.

Where does your attention flag? Where do you find yourself losing the thread of the argument? Which characters feel predictable to you? What excites you or engages you emotionally?

8

Amy Tan

66 The stories I see in music allow my mind to stretch—much in the same way one might stretch a muscle that is cramped. By allowing my imagination to run with the music, it acts as a purgative in clearing my mind of cluttered thoughts. No matter where I am in the world, music is the bringer of reverie. It is not simply pleasure. It is essential.

. . .

I still use music to write scenes. I am embarrassed to admit that I actually have playlists titled 'Joyful,' 'Worried,' 'Hopeful,' 'Destruction,' 'Disaster,' 'Sorrow,' 'Renewal,' and so forth. I choose one track and play it for however long it takes me to finish the scene. It could be hundreds of times. The music ensures that emotion is a constant, even when I am doing the mental work of crafting the story, revising sentences as I go along. It enables me to return to the emotional dream after my focus has been interrupted by barking dogs, doorbells, or my husband bringing me lunch (what a dear man). 🙰

—*Where the Past Begins*

LISTEN

In her memoir, Tan writes about music both in an abstract sense, as a "bringer of reverie," and in very practical terms, using playlists to help her writing. In both cases, it's essential to her practice. Music is unique in its power to convey emotion in an almost universal way. What do you think music can teach us about story?

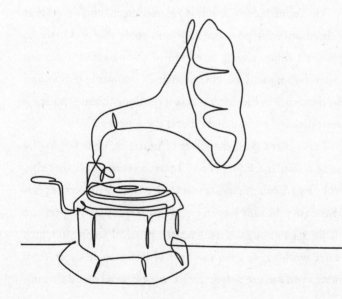

Writing can be a grindingly intellectual activity. Plot, metaphor, characterization—it all takes thought and attention. Here we see Tan express the value of "reverie," a more effortless and wild type of imagination prompted by music. Is reverie a part of your creative practice? Is there a kind of music, or any other trigger, that can bring you into that state of imagination?

WRITE

Tan describes using music as a way to sustain a particular emotional tone in her work, allowing the music to reinforce and echo the feeling she is creating in a particular scene.

Try a similar exercise but in reverse. Begin with a song that feels emotionally powerful to you in some way and listen to it several times, paying attention to the narrative it creates. Listen for repeated snatches of melody, changes in tempo, and the dynamics in the music. As you continue listening, create a short piece of writing that reflects the song itself.

Experiment with the effect of music on your writing by using a similar technique to Tan's and creating playlists that evoke a particular mood as you work to capture it on the page. Music isn't the only way to engage with emotional expression off the page though. Visual art, the physical setting in which you're working, or even the time of day may all be external factors you can use to help create an emotional mood that imbues your writing. How does your writing experience change if you're tucked into an overstuffed chair with flickering candles and soft violin music versus if you're perched on a porch swing in the sun listening to a nostalgic nineties summer playlist?

] 23 [

9

Edith Wharton

· CHARACTER ·

❝ All novelists who describe (whether from without or within) what is called 'society life' are pursued by the idiotic accusation of putting 'real people' (that is, persons actually known to the author) into their books. Anyone gifted with the least creative faculty knows how utterly beside the mark such an accusation is. 'Real people' transported into a work of the imagination would instantly cease to be real; only those born of the creator's brain can give the least illusion of reality.

. . .

No 'character' can be made out of nothing, still less can it be successfully pieced together out of heterogeneous scraps of the 'real,' like dismembered statues of which the fragments have been hopelessly mixed up by the restorer.

. . .

Experience, observation, the looks and ways and words of 'real people,' all melted and fused in the white heat of the creative fires—such is the mingled stuff which the novelist pours into the firm mould of his narrative. **"**

—**"Confessions of a Novelist"**

LISTEN

Regardless of what you're writing, you've probably encountered a friend or family member wondering excitedly if they will be "in" your work—or maybe fearing that they'll show up on the page! Here Wharton briskly lays to rest the idea that writers can simply borrow characters from reality because, in the very act of writing them, they "instantly cease to be real." Do you agree with her? In practical terms, what do you think the difference is between cobbling together a Frankenstein's monster character of mixed parts and creating the "mingled stuff" of a fully reimagined character?

What do Wharton's claims imply for writers of nonfiction? Do you think reporting, biography, or memoir are also, at some level, a creation of fiction or can they accurately reflect their very real subjects?

WRITE

Start by writing down three to five character traits, observations, or features that you've noticed in real life. These can be anything—the unexpectedly intimate scene of a pair of gossiping ladies leaning over their lattes, a stranger's bizarre fashion choice on the subway or in the grocery store parking lot, the meticulous way your brother makes peanut butter crackers—anything you've noticed about another person in the real world that caught your attention.

Use these traits and observations to craft a completely new persona, by writing a brief character sketch *without* mentioning any of the features that first inspired you. Those details are your jumping-off point, but you're now creating a person fully of your imagination. Aim to go beyond what you've observed and envision a whole new personality.

10

Isabel Allende

· LEISURE ·

66 I was always disciplined in my work because I internalized my grandfather's admonition that leisure time was dead time. I followed the rules for decades, but I have learned that leisure can be fertile soil where creativity grows. I am no longer tormented by an excess of discipline, as I was before. Now I write for the pleasure of telling a story word by word, step by step, enjoying the process without thinking of the result. I don't tie myself to a chair eight or ten hours a day, writing with the concentration of a notary.

. . .

I write about what I care for, in my own rhythm. In those leisure hours that my grandfather considered wasted, the ghosts of imagination become well-defined characters. 99

—*The Soul of a Woman*

LISTEN

Much of the writing advice we hear focuses on discipline. And to be sure, if you'd like to write something, it helps to . . . actually write. But here, Allende praises an unexpected ally in creativity—leisure. How did you feel reading this quote? Did it strike you as frivolous or idealistic or did this approach appeal to you?

As you think about your own writing, consider how you've balanced discipline with leisure in the past. Has it worked well? Do you think you need more of either element in your creative practice?

WRITE

Allende's words are a delightful invitation to allow creativity and imagination into your life in a different way. This week, tuck away your papers, close the laptop, and practice leisure.

What would feel like a luxurious use of your time? Don't choose something that's covertly practical; the goal of this exercise is to spend your time indulgently, even if it's only for an hour. Perhaps it's cracking open a new novel, going for a hike, or puttering around the kitchen with a new recipe. Whatever it may be, take some time to unapologetically incorporate leisure as part of your creative practice. Release the expectation that you'll have something to "show" for it—creativity is more nuanced and subtler than that—and just enjoy!

11

Marilynne Robinson

·EXPECTATIONS·

" [Young writers] come to me persuaded that American readers will not tolerate ideas in their fiction. . . . They are good, generous souls working within limits they feel are imposed on them by a public that could not possibly have an interest in writing that ignored these limits—a public they cannot respect.

. . .

But the worst of it is that so long as a writer is working to satisfy imagined expectations that are extraneous to his art as he would otherwise explore and develop it, he is deprived of the greatest reward, which is the full discovery and engagement of his own mind, his own aesthetic powers and resources. So long as a writer is working below the level of her powers, she is depriving the community of readers of a truly good book. And over time a truly good book can enrich literally millions of lives. "

—"Imagination and Community"

LISTEN

Robinson observes that often writers' fears about what readers will enjoy restricts the work they create. Do you think that writing for a reader generally helps or hinders the writing process?

What kind of "imagined expectations" have you internalized about your own writing? Do you think they restrict the kind of writing you can create?

WRITE

What have you wanted to write that you haven't written because of how you feared it would be perceived?

Perhaps it's a more experimental form, perhaps it's something raw and personal, maybe it's bizarre fantasy you think is "too much" for the reader, or diving into a style of writing that you've always been intimidated by.

This week work on writing something that's fearless. Write the way you would if you knew your reader was engaged and curious and kind; the way you would if there were no expectations and no self-consciousness. Trust your reader, trust yourself, and go for it!

12

Jhumpa Lahiri

· WORDS ·

66 I'm constantly hunting for words.

I would describe the process like this: every day I go into the woods carrying a basket. I find words all around: on the trees, in the bushes, on the ground (in reality: on the street, during conversations, while I read). I gather as many as possible. But it's never enough; I have an insatiable appetite.

. . .

At the end of the day the basket is heavy, overflowing. I feel loaded down, wealthy, in high spirits. My words seem more valuable than money. I am like a beggar who finds a pile of gold, a bag of jewels.

But when I come out of the woods, when I see the basket, scarcely a handful of words remain. The majority disappear. They vanish into thin air, they flow like water between my fingers. Because the basket is memory and memory betrays me, memory doesn't hold up.

. . .

Although defeated, I don't feel too discouraged. If anything, I feel even more determined. The next day, I return to the woods. . . . I know that its beauty lies in the act of gathering, not in the result. **99**

—In Other Words

LISTEN

Words are the essential medium of every writer, the basis for everything we create. In her memoir, Lahiri is writing specifically about how she sought, gathered, and lost words as she learned Italian, but her thoughts here apply to all writers. Do you find that the act of writing has made you more fascinated by and attuned to language?

When you think of books written today versus ten, fifty, or a hundred years ago, how do you think our vocabularies and language have shifted over time? Does the way language is changing in the digital world delight you or concern you?

WRITE

The last time anyone asked you to learn a new word (or "improve your vocabulary") the SATs were probably involved and it was likely horrible. This week, recapture the fascination and joy that Lahiri describes here and purposefully explore words.

Pick up a book that is likely to have words that you haven't encountered before. That might mean taking on some Shakespeare or James Joyce, but you could also pick up a young adult novel with new-to-you slang or dive into book on a more specialized topic—perhaps a science memoir or a nature guide.

As you read, be on the lookout for words to tuck into your basket. Highlight! Actually, use a dictionary instead of just thinking, "I *mostly* know what that means." Add words you especially love to a notebook for future reference.

Keep your eyes and ears open for words in your daily life as well—in emails and supermarkets and overheard in coffee shops. Gather and add to your basket, but don't worry too much if a few words slip through the cracks.

13

Chimamanda Ngozi Adichie

· HONESTY ·

" But I will say that fiction is true. This is something my friends who write nonfiction and I argue about all the time. I feel that fiction is much more honest than nonfiction. I know from my limited experience in writing nonfiction, particularly memoir, that in the process of writing I am constantly negotiating different levels of self-censorship and self-protection, and protection of people I love, and sometimes protection of people I don't necessarily care about but I worry that the reader might have biased feelings about. When I write fiction, I don't think about any of that. Radical honesty is possible in fiction. With fictional characters, I don't have to think about protecting anybody. "

—Interview with *Image*

LISTEN

Fiction is often described as not necessarily *real*, but certainly *true*. Here, Adichie goes a step beyond that and explains that, for her, "fiction is much more honest than nonfiction." Do you agree that fiction opens up the possibility of honesty or truth in a unique way? Do you think the knowledge that it's "just a story" allows that honesty or hinders it?

In your own reading, have you encountered examples of the kind of radical honesty that Adichie describes here? Is that something you aspire to—whether it's fiction or nonfiction?

WRITE

Begin by writing a brief, factually true scene that you have personally experienced. Capture all the details that feel significant to you, emotionally, intellectually, artistically.

Now rewrite that same scene as fiction, still aiming to convey the exact same significant details you included in your first version. Your fictionalized version might be fairly similar to the nonfiction edition or it might involve dancing elephants in pointe shoes—whatever it takes to convey the truth of the moment through fiction.

As you write, pay attention to process—which feels more authentic and genuine? When you compare the two finished pieces, side by side, which do you think better conveys the "truth" of the experience to a reader?

14

Louisa May Alcott

· MAKING A LIVING ·

❝ There is no *easy* road to successful authorship; it has to be earned by long & patient labor, many disappointments, uncertainties & trials. Success is often a lucky accident, coming to those who may not deserve it, while others who do have to wait & hope till they have *earned* it. This is the best sort & the most enduring.

. . .

Little Women was written when I was ill, & to prove that I could not write books for girls. The publisher thought it flat, so did I, & neither hoped much for or from it. We found out our mistake, & since then, though I do not enjoy writing 'moral tales' for the young, I do it because it pays well. ❞

—Letter of advice sent to a Miss Churchill (1878)

LISTEN

In this blunt letter to a young reader, Alcott doesn't indulge in starry-eyed visions of the authorial life, but her honesty is refreshing. What kind of writerly advice have you received in your life? Was it helpful, optimistic, out of touch, frustrating, or something else entirely?

We often assume that passion is the prerequisite for creating good work, but Alcott's example contradicts that assumption. She wrote a book that would become beloved by millions because her publisher pushed her to do so. And she continued to write this style of book because it made her a good living. Does Alcott's acknowledgment of the financial reality of writing appeal to you or does it feel disappointing?

WRITE

Our lives are filled with practical forms of writing that we often barely pay attention to—everything from grocery lists to quick text messages. Put aside your larger literary ambitions for a moment, and instead turn your attention to writing something more utilitarian. For Alcott that happened to be cranking out a children's book in two months that is still read over a century later. But for this exercise we can be a little more modest.

Focus on bringing the level of attention and intent you typically reserve for your creative writing pursuits to something that is purely practical—an email, a business letter, some advertising copy, a thank-you note, perhaps detailed directions for a family recipe. These "genres" of writing can teach us about clarity, precision, and care.

15

Edwidge Danticat

·DANGER·

" Create dangerously, for people who read dangerously. This is what I've always thought it meant to be a writer. Writing, knowing in part that no matter how trivial your words may seem, someday, somewhere, someone may risk his or her life to read them. Coming from where I come from, with the history I have—having spent the first twelve years of my life under both dictatorships of Papa Doc and his son, Jean-Claude—this is what I've always seen as the unifying principle among all writers. . . . Somewhere, if not now, then maybe years in the future, a future that we may have yet to dream of, someone may risk his or her life to read us. Somewhere, if not now, then maybe years in the future, we may also save someone's life (or mind) because they have given us a passport, making us honorary citizens of their culture.

. . .

There are many possible interpretations of what it means to create dangerously, and Albert Camus, like the poet Osip

Mandelstam, suggests that it is creating as a revolt against silence, creating when both the creation and the reception, the writing and the reading, are dangerous undertakings, disobedience to a directive. **"**

—*Create Dangerously*

LISTEN

Danticat challenges writers to "create dangerously"—to produce work that is worth someone risking their life to read it. For many of us, the idea of risking one's life to read something feels unfathomable. And yet, as Danticat notes, that experience is ubiquitous throughout history and continues to be the reality of many living today. How do you understand the concept of creating dangerously? How does it change the stakes of creative work?

It can be hard to wrap our mind around the urgency and stakes of Danticat's observations; we think of world-changing literature as written by particular people with particular pedigrees and qualifications. If you're writing a children's book about dapper ducks you may not consider your work all that subversive. And yet, perhaps it is. Consider examples of literature that has been subversive on all scales—whether it was a book that opened your eyes as a child or one that helped to topple a regime. Who wrote these books? What do they have in common and how do they differ?

WRITE

Spend some time journaling and reflecting on what it would mean for you, specifically, to create dangerously in the way Danticat describes. What about your voice, situation, perspective, or experience do you want to speak into the world? This can feel like a dramatic or even a self-important question, but push past your discomfort and really sit with it.

Danticat writes about danger and disruption on the international and political level, but there can be creative danger in how we write and speak honestly to our particular communities, social circles, and families. What kind of writing feels the most dangerous and most true to you? How can you lean into it boldly?

16

Virginia Woolf

· RHYTHM ·

" Style is a very simple matter: it is all *rhythm*. Once you get that, you can't use the wrong words. But on the other hand here am I sitting after half the morning, crammed with ideas, and visions, and so on, and can't dislodge them, for lack of the right rhythm. Now this is very profound, what rhythm is, and goes far deeper than words. A sight, an emotion, creates this wave in the mind, long before it makes words to fit it; and in writing (such is my present belief) one has to recapture this, and set this working (which has nothing apparently to do with words) and then, as it breaks and tumbles in the mind, it makes words to fit it. But no doubt I shall think differently next year. "

—Letter to Vita Sackville-West (1926)

LISTEN

In her letter, Woolf offers a beautiful but elusive vision of the concept of rhythm in writing. It is a core element of style; it transcends words and shapes them to fit its own ends. What does rhythm mean to you in the context that Woolf describes? Have you ever felt the sense of rhythm in your own work?

WRITE

Woolf's insight here is beautiful, but not entirely easy to replicate. It's a comfort to know that Woolf also found herself flummoxed by the "lack of the right rhythm" for her work.

The rhythm Woolf is writing about is deeper than the meaning we traditionally ascribe to that word (after all it "has nothing apparently to do with words"), but nonetheless, poetic rhythm can carry a great deal of emotional meaning and go "far deeper than words."

Spend time with poetry this week—read some of your favorites and writers you've never picked up before. Read their work aloud and focus on the way the language moves and flows as you speak.

Practice writing with a sense of rhythm and meter. If it suits your fancy, you might try poetry, but rhythm is ubiquitous in all writing and language. Think about the jarring staccato dialogue of an angry encounter or the frenetic tattoo of a defensive explanation. If there's a scene you've felt stuck on, reconsider what's working, or not working, through the lens of rhythm.

17

Joy Harjo

· OBJECTS ·

66 When my mother passed, I inherited an iron cooking pot brought over on the Trail that belonged to her mother's mother.

Some of the most important stories are not in words, or in poems or other forms of speaking, but in objects of use and beauty. This cooking pot is one of the most potent stories I carry, made at the end of the century before last, one of many such pots used by Native people east of the Mississippi. The one that was passed through generations of women came to me from my mother. It tells of survival, of the labors of women who cooked, cleaned, and uplifted everyone with stories and songs. The pot is sitting at my feet while I am writing. 99

—*Poet Warrior*

LISTEN

Harjo makes a beautiful point in this quote—sometimes the most eloquent storytellers are "objects of use and beauty." How do you see both the object she's describing and the story it carries working in concert with Harjo's writing in this passage?

Reflect back on objects in your own life that are heavy with stories. In your mind, what sets a story-filled object apart from a simple possession? Time, circumstance, intent, or something else altogether?

WRITE

There's a paradox at the heart of this passage; Harjo is speaking of the storytelling power of an object, but she is also using the written word to share that insight. In writing about the object itself she gives us a reflected glimpse of the story it carries— even if we can't hold the heft of the iron pot ourselves.

Find your own storytelling object and translate its tale into your writing. The object can be something with an apparent story, like a one-way plane ticket, or one that's more deeply hidden, like a simple coffee mug. As you write, aim to keep the focus tightly on the object-as-story. How does its physical presence—shape, weight, color, texture—convey the story? Be sure to capture these physical details in what you write. You want your reader to be able to envision the object as if they're holding it in their own hands.

18

Ann Patchett

·CURIOSITY·

" How other people live life is pretty much all I think about. Curiosity is the rock upon which fiction is built. But for all the times people have wanted to tell me their story because they think it would make a wonderful novel, it pretty much never works out. People are not characters, no matter how often we tell them they are; conversations are not dialogue; and the actions of our days don't add up to a plot. In life, time runs along in its sameness, but in fiction time is condensed—one action springboards into another, greater action. Cause and effect are so much clearer in novels than in life. You might not see how everything threads together as you read along, but when you look back from the end of the story, the map becomes clear. "

—*These Precious Days: Essays*

LISTEN

Patchett observes that novels have clearer lines of cause and effect than the meandering threads of real life. How does this more clearly delineated causality change the way readers approach fiction?

Do you agree with Patchett that "the actions of our days don't add up to a plot"—what do you think is the transforming ingredient between real life and plot?

WRITE

First off, accept this brilliant permission from Patchett *not* to write about your great-aunt's harrowing experience on a bus in downtown Cincinnati, no matter how many times she tells you it was the stuff of legend.

Now that you're free from that, let's focus on dialogue. Borrow some dialogue from a real life—perhaps overheard in a coffee shop, lifted from the family dinner table, or swiped from a pair of joggers in the park. Write down what is said word for word as best you can. You might notice it's a bit meandering, repetitive, or involves more nothing words (murmurs of agreement, mm-hmms, etc.) than you would have thought.

After reading through the transcript, put it aside and re-write that dialogue the way you would for a story. Stay true to the content of the conversation, but make it tighter, faster paced, and more dynamic. Allow each sentence and comment to, as Patchett observed, springboard into the next.

19

Maxine Hong Kingston

·POWER·

" Writing is an act of nonviolence, but it's very active, very aggressive, but you're not setting off bombs or guns. Just using the pen. It's like shouting and getting your voice heard and the range is worldwide. You might not be able to stop a war right now, but the words can go out and influence the atmosphere and the world, way into the future. **"**

—Interview with the *Los Angeles Review of Books*

LISTEN

Prevailing wisdom often categorizes words as passive—"actions speak louder than words," as they say. Yet here, Kingston describes writing as a "very active, very aggressive" "act of nonviolence." Does that description surprise you? Do you agree with her characterization?

Thinking through what you've read personally, have you encountered books or authors that capture the strength and passion that Kingston describes here? What about these works makes their writing feel "like shouting" in a good way?

WRITE

Take some time this week and consider what you want your writing to accomplish. Understanding the *why* behind your writing will equip you to make decisions about the craft of the writing itself. Your goals certainly don't have to be focused on social or political change, nor do you have to be aiming to be published around the globe in order to have a powerful voice. Regardless of whether you're writing a bedtime story for your niece or a novel that you hope will shift a cultural conversation, be honest and curious about your own hopes and dreams for your writing as you think about Kingston's advice and respond to the questions below.

Who do you want to read your work?

How do you want your reader to feel as they read your work?

Is there a core idea or concept that you want readers to absorb when they read your work?

How do you want readers to respond to what you create?

If you knew that you would be listened to, that your voice would be heard, what would you write?

20

Jean Rhys

· GIVE AND TAKE ·

66 All of writing is a huge lake. There are great rivers that feed the lake, like Tolstoy or Dostoyevsky. And then there are trickles, like Jean Rhys. All that matters is feeding the lake. . . . It is very important. Nothing else is important. . . . But you now should be taking from the lake before you can think of feeding it. You must dig your bucket in very deep. . . . What matters is the lake. And man's unconquerable mind. 99

—"Jean Rhys: A Remembrance"

LISTEN

Does Rhys's metaphor of "feeding the lake" feel encouraging or daunting to you as you consider your own writing? How can being part of this vast whole—"all of writing"—be interpreted as a kind of freedom?

In the second part of this quote, Rhys reminds us that all writers need to be nourished by the work of others, to be "taking from the lake." Are there situations where you find the creativity of others to be intimidating instead of inspiring? How can you change that perspective?

WRITE

Rhys's wisdom here is exceptionally freeing, so take it as license to feed the lake however you wish. First read deeply and joyfully in whatever genre delights you—from beach reads to postmodernist theory—and then just write. No agenda, no exercises, no word counts, no rules.

Write free and loose, or slowly and thoughtfully. Just write. Throw a few raindrops of your own in the lake and celebrate the freedom of being part of an enormous, ever-growing literary legacy.

21

George Eliot

· FREEDOM ·

“ Happily, we are not dependent on argument to prove that Fiction is a department of literature in which women can, after their kind, fully equal men. A cluster of great names, both living and dead, rush to our memories in evidence that women can produce novels not only fine, but among the very finest—novels, too, that have a precious specialty, lying quite apart from masculine aptitudes and experience. No educational restrictions can shut women out from the materials of fiction, and there is no species of art which is so free from rigid requirements. Like crystalline masses, it may take any form, and yet be beautiful; we have only to pour in the right elements—genuine observation, humor, and passion. ”

—Silly Novels by Lady Novelists

LISTEN

Eliot celebrates the unique accessibility of writing—anyone, from any background, can be a writer and bring their own voice and form to the work. Yet, as Eliot herself encountered throughout her career, there are certainly gatekeepers in the literary world. Do you think that writing, by virtue of its ability to "take any form," is more accessible to diverse creators than other forms of art? Has that been your experience?

Eliot identifies three elements, "genuine observation, humor, and passion," that are the heart of fiction. If you were to distill good writing or good fiction down to three key elements, what would they be?

WRITE

Eliot observes that fiction, in particular, is free from "rigid requirements" and is not restricted to any particular form. Explore the idea of rethinking form by trying a new approach to your writing.

Pick a form or technique you've always admired or been curious about—perhaps a dual narrative, first-person voice, an unreliable narrator, or epistolary structure—and try it out. As you write, consider the utility of the particular style you're trying out. Does it allow you to get closer to your narrator? To introduce a new plot element? Change the pace of the writing? Be observant and curious.

If you're working on a larger novel or collection, and find yourself stuck, try tackling it in a different way by changing the form—switch the voice, write it like a screenplay or children's novel, imagine it as a flashback, whatever helps you approach it. Even if this exercise never sees the light of day, it will spark your creativity and give you a new approach.

22

Sandra Cisneros

· AUDIENCE ·

❝ She *doesn't* want to write a book that a reader won't understand and would feel ashamed for not understanding.

. . .

She thinks people who are busy working for a living deserve beautiful little stories, because they don't have much time and are often tired. She has in mind a book that can be opened at any page and will still make sense to the reader who doesn't know what came before or comes after.

She experiments, creating a text that is as succinct and flexible as poetry, snapping sentence into fragments so that the reader pauses, making each sentence serve *her* and not the other way around, abandoning quotation marks to streamline the typography and make the page as simple and readable as possible. So that the sentences are pliant as branches and can be read in more ways than one. **❞**

—Introduction to the twenty-fifth-anniversary edition of
The House on Mango Street (Cisneros is writing in the third person
here, describing the person she was when she wrote the book)

LISTEN

Cisneros began her work for *The House on Mango Street* by envisioning a reader—someone who is "busy working for a living" and is "often tired." Her affection for that reader and her desire to give them the "beautiful little stories" they deserve determined the form of her writing. How do you see form and audience intersecting?

Writers are often chided and told to write to the market (meaning to write what is popular and selling well at the moment) and then conversely cautioned to *never, ever* write to the market. Is there a difference between writing to the market and writing for a specific reader?

WRITE

Not all writers have such a clear vision of their reader in mind, but, inspired by Cisneros, spend some time envisioning your reader. Who are they? For this exercise, write your reader as a character. Try to push past basic demographic information (female readers ages twenty-five to forty-five) and envision your reader as a fully fleshed-out person. Who are they? What is their backstory? What kind of writing thrills them? What led them to pick up your work?

23

Flannery O'Connor

· REALITY ·

❝ One of the most common and saddest spectacles is that of a person of really fine sensibility and acute psychological perception trying to write fiction by using these qualities alone. This type of writer will put down one intensely emotional or keenly perceptive sentence after the other, and the result will be complete dullness. The fact is that the materials of the fiction writer are the humblest. Fiction is about everything human and we are made out of dust, and if you scorn getting yourself dusty, then you shouldn't try to write fiction. It's not a grand enough job for you.

Now when the fiction writer finally gets this idea through his head and into his habits, he begins to realize what a job of heavy labor the writing of fiction is. ❞

—*Mystery and Manners: Occasional Prose*

LISTEN

Do you agree with O'Connor that works of fiction that focus solely on "keenly perceptive" insights or intense emotion end up being dull? What makes a piece of writing engaging for you personally?

What do you think it means to "[get] yourself dusty" in writing? Are there authors you think embody O'Connor's vision of writing?

WRITE

O'Connor argues for a style of writing that is physically grounded and doesn't shy away from the dust and grit of reality. This kind of humble, human-scale writing often comes down to details—the physical minutiae of a scene, the way that piece of writing appeals to the reader's five senses to give texture and reality to an idea.

Practice writing in a way that is concretely grounded by focusing on the five senses. Write a scene that shows the reader a physical experience of touch, taste, scent, sound, or vision. What does it *feel* like in the moment you're writing?

Begin by envisioning yourself in the scene and simply noting down all of the sensations and impressions that are involved in that location—everything from the heat of the sun to the smoothness of the floor to the dust hanging in the air. Close your eyes (even if that feels silly) and imagine that experience. What does it physically feel like to exist in the moment you want to write about? Jot down everything that you experience and imagine. Select a few details from this list of impressions, whatever best creates the scene and will help your reader envision the experience, and incorporate them into your writing.

24

Octavia Butler

· IMPEDIMENTS ·

" Here are some potential impediments for you to forget about:

First forget *inspiration*. Habit is more dependable. Habit will sustain you whether you're inspired or not. Habit will help you finish and polish your stories. Inspiration won't. Habit is persistence in practice.

Forget *talent*. If you have it, fine. Use it. If you don't have it, it doesn't matter. As habit is more dependable than inspiration, continued learning is more dependable than talent. Never let pride or laziness prevent you from learning, improving your work, and changing its direction when necessary.

. . .

Finally, don't worry about imagination. You have all the imagination you need . . . and the learning you will be doing will stimulate it. Play with your ideas. Have fun with them. Don't worry about being silly or outrageous or wrong. So much of writing is fun. It's first letting your interest and your imagination take you anywhere at all. Once you're able to do that, you'll have more ideas than you can use. Then the real work of fashioning them into a story begins. Stay with it. Persist. **"**

—"Furor Scribendi"

LISTEN

Butler's first piece of advice, that habit is more dependable than inspiration, is one you might have heard before. But her next two points—that talent and imagination are *not* the key to good writing—are more surprising. How do you think about talent and imagination? Do you believe Butler that learning and playfulness are more reliable ways to create?

WRITE

Instead of the elusive ideas of inspiration, talent, and imagination, Butler advises habit, continued learning, and fun. This

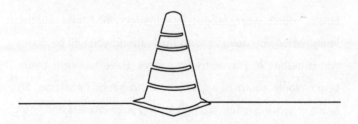

week, take some time to try Butler's prescription of continued learning.

Consider a subject you've always been curious about—regardless of whether or not it relates to your writing—and go learn about it. What are you interested in? Poultry? Ancient architecture? The rise of reality television? It might be related to your writing work or something completely different; just make sure you're genuinely interested in the subject. Dive in and learn! Take yourself on a library field trip and check out some books. Hop online and plumb the depths of YouTube. Tumble down a cascade of Wikipedia articles. Follow your curiosity wherever it might lead you. Let learning take the place of talent for the week.

25

Elena Ferrante

· TRADITION ·

" I wouldn't recognize myself without women's strug-
gles, women's nonfiction writing, women's literature: they
made me an adult. My experience as a novelist, both published
and unpublished, culminated after twenty years, in the attempt to relate, with writing that was appropriate, my sex
and its difference. But for a long time I've thought that if we
have to cultivate *our* narrative tradition, we should never
renounce the stock of techniques that we have behind us.
We have to demonstrate, precisely because we are women,
that we can construct worlds as wide and powerful and rich
as those designed by male writers, if not more. So we have
to be well equipped, we have to dig deep into our difference, using advanced tools. Above all we mustn't give up our
greatest freedom. . . . Writing requires maximum ambition,
maximum audacity, and programmatic disobedience. **"**

—"Women Who Write"

LISTEN

Ferrante alludes to the legacy of female writers and how they've shaped her understanding of her own work and how she creates it. How have you been shaped by the work of particular writers?

What do you think it means to "dig deep into our difference"? What is *your* difference? How can you implement it in your work?

WRITE

Pick a technique or style inspired by one of your favorite female authors, from the "stock of techniques" these brilliant writers have left behind, and practice using it in your own work. This could be something very specific (the way Emily Dickinson uses the em dash like a switchblade) or more general (how Elena Ferrante captures a unique, vivid sense of place in her writing).

Read their work and pay close, specific attention to what makes you love a piece of writing. You know you appreciate the result of their writing, but what is the *how* behind it? It can be helpful to focus on a short passage or section so that you can analyze it more closely. What can you replicate and try out in your own work?

Select one of the methods you observed and put it into practice in your own writing. It can be as short as a few practice sentences just to catch the feel, but give it a try!

26

Roxane Gay

· TRAUMA ·

❝ When you're finally ready to write about trauma, there is a temptation to offer up your testimony, to transcribe all the brutal details as if that is the whole of the work that needs to be done. There is a temptation to indulge not so much in writing but in confession. Sometimes suffering becomes more bearable when you can share the whole truth of it.

Not all writing about trauma is created equal. As with most subjects, writers can be careless with trauma. They can be solipsistic. They can write concerned only with what they need to say and not with what an audience might need to hear. They assume their trauma, in and of itself, is the only story they need to tell, or that having experienced trauma is inherently interesting. Or trauma serves as pornography—a way of titillating the reader, a lazy way of creating narrative tension, as if it is only through suffering that we have a story to tell. We see trauma as it unfolds but are rarely given a broader understanding of that trauma or its after-math. **99**

—*Writing into the Wound*

LISTEN

Gay highlights a difference between confession and writing. What strikes you as the separation between those two modes? Is there overlap between them?

What do you think it means to be "careless with trauma" as a writer? What effect does that have both on the reader and the writer?

WRITE

Trauma can be broadly defined; it might refer to something deeply personal and painful you've experienced or to a collective experience such as living through a global pandemic or experiencing discrimination based on race or gender. Reflect on Gay's quote here and, if you feel comfortable, write something in this space of suffering.

Regardless of whether you would use the word trauma to describe the experience you're writing about, think of this as an invitation to write something personal and close to the

bone. As you write, consider your experience as a writer—
the confessional aspects, the way that giving voice to an experience can be a relief—without losing sight of your reader
(even if another soul never lays eyes on what you've written)
and how you can convey a broader meaning through relating
a specific experience. Don't be afraid to dive deeply into your
writing, but remember to be gentle with both yourself and
your reader.

27

Louise Erdrich

· JUST WRITE ·

" I would not think about appearances; I would just write. I would not think about whether I had a good idea; I would just write it. I would not think about whether I was capable; I would just put my pen on the page. And if I had an idea at any point and I was tired, I would write it anyway. And that's one of the hardest things to do for me. You know, you're doing something else, you're exhausted. Wake up in the middle of the night. You gotta write. You can't give yourself an out. I didn't give myself an out. It was never easy to do, but on the other hand, I really love doing it. It's not like it's work, exactly. You just can't let yourself argue with your writer. You have to listen to the writer at all times. And that's all I can say. "

—Interview with *Otherppl*

LISTEN

What do you think Erdrich means when she talks about not focusing on appearances? How can appearances—of our work, our lives, our own viewpoints as writers—become a hindrance?

Erdrich's advice here isn't necessarily unexpected, but it's worth reiterating. How do you "give yourself an out"? How can you make different choices to confront your work bravely instead of shying away?

WRITE

If there's something you've convinced yourself you're not capable of tackling in your writing, now is the time! You already know exactly what this is, the part you've been avoiding. It might be the ending you know is going to be tricky to get right, the scene you're not sure how to bring together, the hard, honest bit of your memoir your family is going to hate, the idea you secretly adore but are intimidated by. Whatever the difficult thing is, now is the time to tackle it. You've got this, just write it!

28

Jane Smiley

· ROUGH DRAFTS ·

“ What your rough draft contains is the whole system of the story you have been thinking about, the choices you've made and the other possible choices, too. . . . You have had feelings, intuitions, observations, perceptions, and ideas that are not written down but that have been part of your mind while you were working on and around this rough draft. The rough draft as it stands harkens toward these more shadowy parts of the story, and they will be available to you if you can recognize their presence. But since they are shadowy, you have to develop a heightened sensitivity to what is in your rough draft; you have to be receptive to what you have written as if your memories of writing . . . are not significant. The art of revision lies in not pressing your self upon the story. The story has now made the first step in separating itself from you. It will not live unless it separates itself from you entirely, and it can't do that unless you are receptive to what it is trying to be. ”

—"What Stories Teach Their Writers"

LISTEN

What do you think Smiley means when she writes about a story needing to separate itself from you entirely? Does her way of personifying a piece of writing feel foreign to you or does it resonate with how you think of your work?

The kind of revision that Smiley suggests here requires writers to gain some distance from their own writing—to see what the work is doing apart from what they think it *ought* to be doing or what they *intended* for it to do. As a writer, how do you think you can gain that kind of emotional and intellectual distance?

WRITE

Keeping in mind Smiley's concept of separation, read through a rough draft of your own work. As much as possible, read your work the way you would read that of another writer. This is hard! Ask yourself what this piece is trying to accomplish and how it is going about it. Let the words on the page answer those questions, instead of jumping in with what you, as the author, assume are the answers.

As you read, what themes, concepts, and ideas stand out to you? What is emphasized and what is repeated? What is downplayed or avoided? As you revise, set aside what you *think* the story should be saying and lean into the elements you've just observed. How can they be strengthened and honed to serve the work?

29

Jane Austen

· CONTRAST ·

" Upon the whole, however, I am quite vain enough and well satisfied enough. The work is rather too light, and bright, and sparkling: it wants shade; it wants to be stretched out here and there with a long chapter of sense, if it could be had; if not, of solemn specious nonsense, about something unconnected with the story; an essay on writing, a critique on Walter Scott, or the history of Buonaparté or something that would form a contrast, and bring the reader with increased delight to the playfulness and epigramma-tism of the general style. "

—Letter to her sister Cassandra (1813)

LISTEN

Since Austen's letters were burned after her death, we have precious little writerly advice from her. But Austen's rather tongue-in-cheek evaluation of *Pride and Prejudice* survives today. What do you make of her critique that the book is "rather too light and bright and sparkling"?

WRITE

Adding an essay on writing or an involved history of Buonaparté to the middle of your novel might not quite be the best editing advice, but sarcasm aside, Austen raises an intriguing idea about contrast. A shift in voice or content can be particularly revealing—whether it's a moment of levity in a dark tale or sudden note of seriousness in a lighthearted one.

In good Austenian fashion, write a letter that makes use of this concept of contrast. That might mean a noticeable shift in diction, from genial and informal to elevated and academic; in structure, from long, convoluted sentences to staccato ones; or in tone, shifting from pensive and emotional to "light and bright and sparkling." Notice how the change, however brief, highlights the style and method of the rest of the writing.

30

Maya Angelou

· WORKING ·

“ I try to pull the language in to such a sharpness that it jumps off the page. It must look easy, but it takes me forever to get it to look so easy. Of course, there are those critics— New York critics as a rule—who say, Well, Maya Angelou has a new book out and of course it's good but then she's a natural writer. Those are the ones I want to grab by the throat and wrestle to the floor because it takes me forever to get it to sing. I *work* at the language.

. . .

When I would end up writing after four hours or five hours in my room, it might sound like, It was a rat that sat on a mat. That's that. Not a cat. But I would continue to play with it and pull at it and say, I love you. Come to me. I love you. It might take me two or three weeks just to describe what I'm seeing now. ”

—**Interview with *The Paris Review* in *Women Writers at Work***

LISTEN

We oftentimes encounter a narrative around creativity that implies some people have that special je ne sais quoi that makes writing come easily for them. But here, Angelou rejects the label of a "natural writer" and the idea of effortless perfection, insisting that she has to work hard for the words and language. She prefers to be recognized for the labor she puts into her work. How is that claim countercultural or unexpected? How do you personally think of the intersection of talent or skill and work?

What do you think it means, in concrete terms, to "work at the language"?

WRITE

Angelou is honest that, when she begins, the work she creates is ... bad. It takes courage and patience to sit with bad writing

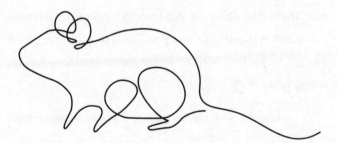

and coax it into something better, but that's exactly what Angelou encourages us to try. Take a section of your own writing that is at the"it was a rat that sat on a mat" stage and settle down to make it sing.

Start with a small section—a few paragraphs or lines—and begin by reading it through closely. Pay attention to all the parts that make you cringe and want to delete your hard drive or throw your notebook under a truck. Some things to consider:

- What about this section of writing do you hate? Where is the language off? Highlight or underline the specific sections or sentences that are not working.
- Now begin to dissect *why* these sections are not reading well. Consider the length and cadence of your sentences, the metaphors you're using, the rhythm of the dialogue. Don't cave and delete the whole thing—take the time to figure out what is not working.
- Now that you have a sense of the problem, start doing the work to fix it. Take inspiration from Angelou and approach this task with a sense of playfulness and even love. Invite a better word, a cleverer sentence, a gentle observation. Be patient—it takes time to make words sing.

31

Anne Lamott

· DIALOGUE ·

❝ First of all, sound your words—read them out loud. If you can't bring yourself to do this, mouth your dialogue. This is something you have to practice, doing it over and over.

. . .

Second, remember that you should be able to identify each character by what he or she says. Each one must sound different from the others. And they should not all sound like you; each one must have a self.

. . .

Third, you might want to try putting together two people who more than anything else in the world wish to avoid each other, people who would avoid whole cities just to make sure they won't bump into each other. ❞

—*Bird by Bird*

LISTEN

How does reading something out loud shift your perception of it?

What elements of dialogue do you think make a character's voice unique and distinct from other characters? Thinking through the work of some of your favorite writers, how do they accomplish what Lamott describes in her second suggestion?

WRITE

Take Lamott's third piece of advice and try writing a scene that forces two characters who truly, deeply detest each other into proximity. The characters don't need to be forced together for any particularly dramatic reason—their dynamic and dialogue will create more than enough friction.

Envision a scenario in which your characters are so tightly wound they finally reach the point of saying what they truly mean to each other—and let the dialogue flow!

32

Zora Neale Hurston

· URGENCY ·

" I wrote *Their Eyes Were Watching God* in Haiti. It was dammed up in me, and I wrote it under internal pressure in seven weeks. I wish that I could write it again. In fact, I regret all of my books. It is one of the tragedies of life that one cannot have all the wisdom one is ever to possess in the beginning. Perhaps, it is just as well to be rash and foolish for a while. If writers were too wise, perhaps no books would get written at all. It might be better to ask yourself "Why?" afterwards than before. Anyway, the force from somewhere in Space which commands you to write in the first place, gives you no choice. You take up the pen when you are told, and write what is commanded. There is no agony like bearing an untold story inside you. You have all heard of the Spartan youth with the fox under his cloak. "

—*Dust Tracks on a Road*

LISTEN

Hurston writes with blunt honesty that she regrets all of her books. At the same time she's matter-of-fact about that regret, positing that it might be "just as well to be rash and foolish" or else nothing might get written in the first place. Does knowing that a celebrated and gifted writer like Hurston carried feelings of regret for her writing feel freeing or daunting to you? Do you agree that an element of foolishness might be a key ingredient in putting words on the page?

If you're not familiar with the rather grisly tale of the Spartan boy and the fox, it recounts how on his way to school a boy saw a fox kit and decided to keep it as a pet. He hid it under his cloak and continued on to school. The fox grew restless and frightened and started biting and gnawing at the boy under his cloak. Rather than draw attention to the kit he'd smuggled into class, the boy sat stoically throughout the day until he fell down dead, mauled to death by the fox. What does Hurston's reference to this peculiarly grim anecdote reveal about her experience of creativity? Have you experienced a similar kind of urgency in your own creative life?

WRITE

Oftentimes we have writing work we feel we should do, but are tempted to "cheat" on our main project with an appealing new idea. Give yourself permission to take a break from what you "should" be writing in order to pursue whatever feels most urgent to you. There's a reason that new idea is snagging your attention, so see where it takes you. Set aside some time, whether it's half an hour or an afternoon, to pursue whatever writing demands your attention.

That might be a long-winded letter to someone who needs setting straight, a poem sparked by a particular slant of light out your window, or a meandering scene for your novel that's been kicking around your head. Even if you don't feel you have something "dammed up" that you must start writing, follow the thread of your interest and see where it takes you.

33

Annie Dillard

·MATERIALITY·

" The materiality of the writer's life cannot be exaggerated. If you like metaphysics, throw pots. How fondly I recall thinking in the old days, that to write you needed paper, pen, and a lap. How appalled I was to discover that, in order to write so much as a sonnet, you need a warehouse. You can easily get so confused writing a thirty-page chapter that in order to make an outline for the second draft, you have to rent a hall. I have often 'written' with the mechanical aid of a twenty-foot conference table. You lay your pages along the table's edge and pace out the work. You walk along the rows; you weed bits, move bits, and dig out bits, bent over the rows with full hands like a gardener. After a couple of hours you have taken an exceedingly dull nine-mile hike. You go home and soak your feet. "

—*The Writing Life*

LISTEN

Dillard cheerfully dispels any visions of writing as a lofty pursuit of the mind and reminds us that being a good writer involves taking some "exceedingly dull" hikes (whether literally or figuratively) in the name of good editing. Do you tend to think of writing as a purely intellectual pursuit? What has your experience been of "the materiality of the writer's life"?

WRITING

Many of us rely on more digital methods of writerly work than Dillard describes here, but there's something incredibly valuable about seeing a chapter or essay physically present. Whether or not you have a warehouse or twenty-foot conference table at your disposal, give Dillard's method a try.

Print out your work (with page numbers!) and arrange the pages in order. Move things around and see how it reads. Is the "end" really the end? Does the middle of the narrative drag? What happens if you remove the slow bits altogether?

If you're reluctant to print everything out or you're working on something too long for this method, you can try a similar technique by writing down the major themes or sections on sticky notes, lining them up on a wall or table, and arranging and rearranging them.

34

Julia Alvarez

· DISCOVERY ·

" Writers write not because they know things but because they want to find things out. And not just informational things—emotional ones, the whole landscape of human feeling, emotion and passion. They want to experience things. They want to discover. Frost said, 'No surprise for the writer, no surprise for the reader.' If you're not discovering, your words will die on the page. "

—"Julia Alvarez Interview: In the Time of Discovery"

LISTEN

Do you agree with Alvarez that without an element of discovery "your words will die on the page"?

When you write, is there something you continually find yourself looking to discover? Do you gravitate to emotional discoveries? Intellectual ones? What fascinates and excites you about writing?

WRITE

The key to discovering is curiosity—not just curiosity about the subject you've chosen to write about, but curiosity about the process of writing, about the writing itself, about the way your words can shift and evolve and grow.

Practice the art of discovering by asking why. Write out a brief scene of mundane action—a postal worker dropping off a package, a cashier scanning toilet paper at a supermarket, a kid playing in the park—whatever comes to mind. Then ask yourself: Why is this happening? Answer that "why" however you like and adjust your scene accordingly. Then ask yourself why again. Answer as imaginatively as you'd like and add these details to your story. Repeat this process—asking why and diving a little bit deeper each time, discovering a little bit more with each question—until your simple little scene has evolved into something altogether different.

35

Nnedi Okorafor

· THE BLANK PAGE ·

❝ This is a battle I fight when beginning a new story when facing the dreaded blank page. There's a voice in my head saying, 'There's nothing there! How can you create something from nothing? Where do I begin? There's no instruction manual or guide I can Google.' That blank page is like the opponent who has everything to gain from me and nothing to lose.

Though I feel this fear every time, I have never walked away from it. I stand and face the monster, then I dance with it and it is exhilarating. 'If you fear something you give it power over you,' says a North African proverb. And if you conquer that fear, you are rewarded with power and joy. ❞

—"The Sport of Writing"

LISTEN

What do you think Okorafor means when she compares the empty page to "an opponent who has everything to gain from me and nothing to lose"? What do you have to lose as a writer? What do you have to gain?

Do you find a blank page intimidating when you sit down to write? How can you shift your perspective of any empty page from intimidation to opportunity?

WRITE

The blank page can be universally intimidating for writers—no matter how successful they may be. Sometimes the easiest way to get over this fear is simply to dive in. For this exercise, grab an actual pen and paper instead of using a computer.

Set a timer for ten minutes, then pick up your pen and write continuously. The goal is to chase the flow of your thoughts and write without stopping, not worrying about editing or structure or perfection.

The topic can be anything you choose, but if you work better with an assigned prompt, here you go: write about unexpected surprises. (Birthday parties, parking tickets, rainstorms, anything unanticipated!)

Write for the sake of writing and vanquish the blank page!

36

Emily Dickinson

· FEELING ·

" If I read a book [and] it makes my whole body so cold no fire can ever warm me, I know that is poetry. If I feel physically as if the top of my head were taken off, I know that is poetry. These are the only ways I know it. Is there any other way? "

—Letter to Thomas Wentworth Higginson (1870)

LISTEN

Have you ever experienced something like what Dickinson described? What work of literature, or other type of art, has thrilled and electrified you in a similar way?

WRITE

What does it feel like when you read something powerful and transformative? What are the ways you "know it" as Dickinson does? Write about the experience of reading and how it feels to you—physically, emotionally, intellectually, or whichever way you "feel" writing that connects with you.

Keep this description as inspiration and encouragement to write in such a way that you inspire that reaction in *your* readers.

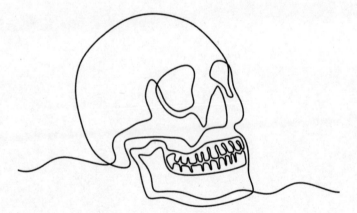

37

N. K. Jemisin

· MYTH ·

66 My inspiration is usually mythology. I'm more interested in stories as they've existed throughout antiquity. I
like oral storytelling; I like creation myths of various peoples
and cultures and religions. I myself am an agnostic, so I see
all religions and all creation myths as mythology, although
I know that for a lot of people it's a lived experience. As far
as I am concerned, humanity has had several thousand years
to perfect storytelling, and there's a lot to be learned from
those basic, classic—even primordial—storytelling forms and
ideologies. That is more interesting to me than what is selling best and what is popular. 99

—Interview with the Odyssey Writing Workshop

LISTEN

Jemisin observes that "humanity has had several thousand years to perfect storytelling." What do you think modern storytellers can learn from this inherited tradition?

It's interesting to remember that storytelling long predates writing. How do you think oral traditions versus the written word influence the kind of stories we tell and the way those stories are structured?

WRITE

Find a myth, fable, or traditional story that intrigues you, and use it as a jumping-off point to write your own story. It could be a Russian fairy tale, a Mesopotamian creation myth, an Indian epic poem—any traditional story that catches your attention.

These kinds of tales are deeply captivating because they reflect universal human experiences or concerns, but they're often sparse on details, creating a perfect framework for you to play with.

Consider changing the time period or cultural context, explore the background of a secondary character, create a fully fleshed-out context for the protagonist, or write from the perspective of the antagonist. Rewrite and reimagine the original myth until you've created something altogether new!

38

Elizabeth Gilbert

· CREATIVITY ·

    " In contemporary Western civilization, the most common creative contract still seems to be one of suffering. This is the contract that says, *I shall destroy myself and everyone around me in an effort to bring forth my inspiration, and my martyrdom shall be the badge of my creative legitimacy.*

    . . .

A different way is to cooperate fully, humbly, and joyfully with inspiration.

    . . .

You can receive your ideas with respect and curiosity, not with drama or dread. You can clear out whatever obstacles are preventing you from living your most creative life, with the simple understanding that whatever is bad for you is probably also bad for your work. . . . You can battle your demons (through therapy, recovery, prayer, or humility) instead of battling your gifts—in part by realizing that your demons were never the ones doing the work anyhow. You can believe you are neither a slave to inspiration nor its master, but something far more interesting—its partner—and that the two of you are working together toward something intriguing and worthwhile. **,,**

—Big Magic

LISTEN

Have you encountered the contract of suffering that Gilbert describes here? Why do you think the image of the tortured artist is so culturally captivating?

What does it look like for you personally when you're battling your gifts instead of your demons?

WRITE

Oftentimes we think of inspiration as something elusive and fickle, something we have to woo or maybe even chase and crush in our fists so it never escapes. Gilbert offers a much more appealing vision of a partnership with inspiration. Let's explore what that partnership might look like.

Start by noticing a spark of inspiration in your daily life this week. This doesn't have to be the seed of an epic novel or world-changing exposé (though if it is, run with it!), just something that sparks your interest and catches your eye.

Perhaps a weird science fact (jellyfish can technically be immortal), something visually beautiful (grocery store bouquets, Monet), an interesting relationship dynamic (every family in existence).

Before you sit down to write about your inspiration, spend some time with it the way you would with any partner. Mull it over, ask it questions, consider its context, play around with the idea. You're not interrogating your inspiration and insisting it cough up some meaning, you're taking it out for coffee and having a nice chat.

At the end of the week, once you've had some time to get to know each other, sit down with your inspiration and do some writing together. Maybe it's a short story, maybe it's a character study, maybe it's a haiku. Whatever results, trust the partnership and follow where it leads you.

39

Han Kang

· QUESTIONS ·

" Writing is a way of questioning for me. I don't try to find an answer, but to complete the question, or to stay within the question as long as I can. In a sense, writing fiction can be compared with pacing back and forth. You go forward and then come back again, pondering questions that both sear and chill you internally. **"**

—*Banana Writers* interview

LISTEN

Kang says that "in a sense, writing fiction can be compared with pacing back and forth." Why do you think she chooses to compare fiction to pacing instead of the more common metaphor of a journey?

In your own writing, do you find that you are often trying to find an answer or are you content to simply pursue a question? As a reader, do you prefer one style of writing over the other?

WRITE

Ask a question that "both sear[s] and chill[s] you internally." You might know immediately what this question is or you might need to ponder in order to find it. It could be a deeply personal question about yourself or your family or a broad societal one. Choose a question that makes you feel a throb of emotion, possibly one that makes you want to shy away and not look closer.

Write your question at the top of a page and spend some time exploring it. You don't need to come to a conclusive answer. As Kang observes, there is profound value in staying with the question wherever it may lead and many times that journey of exploration is more valuable than a tidy answer.

You might explore the question through story, in poetry, or simply in a cascade of related questions. It might simply be a barrage of words or a mind map that relates, somehow, to the question you're considering. The goal here is to start from a place of emotion and have the courage to dig deeper, to pace and wrestle and explore both the emotion and the question that causes it.

40

Nadia Hashimi

· UNIVERSAL AND PARTICULAR ·

> **"** I set out to reflect a universal point of friction—women struggling for agency within a home, for free will within her own head, for a place within history—but within an Afghan context.
>
> To write these stories with any authenticity is to write with abandon. I write characters who bear traits I've seen in vivo: flawed, inconsistent, forgivable, inspiring, damaged, human. I summon the granular stories told and retold in our family, the spectrum of glorious and devastating experiences. **"**

—**"On Writing Flawed, Inconsistent, Forgivable, Inspiring, and Damaged Afghan Characters"**

LISTEN

Hashimi writes that telling stories "with any authenticity is to write with abandon." What do you think that means? How does authenticity connect with freedom and ease?

How do you think the universal and particular should connect in writing? Are there writers that you think balance them especially well?

WRITE

Hashimi beautifully describes the duality of writing—of starting with "a universal point of friction" and bringing it to life through "granular stories." This move from the broad to the particular and vice versa is at the heart of storytelling.

This week, deliberately practice this shift. Begin with a widely applicable question that interests you. It might be about interpersonal relationships, a philosophical question, or a particular injustice like those Hashimi explores. This is your starting point.

Now, consider this Big Picture question through the smaller context of individual stories and experiences. How have you seen this issue affect individuals? What does it look like in real life, "in vivo"? How can you embody and explore it through specific situations? What experiences have you lived, in your own particular context, that provide a lens for understanding the larger issue?

You can also explore this exercise in reverse: starting with a small experience or moment and following it back to its larger, more universal roots.

41

Cheryl Strayed

· THE GROUND FLOOR ·

" Buried beneath all the anxiety and sorrow and fear and self-loathing, there's arrogance at its core. It presumes you *should* be successful at twenty-six, when really it takes most writers so much longer to get there. . . . You loathe yourself, and yet you're consumed by the grandiose ideas you have about your own importance. You're up too high and down too low. Neither is the place where we get any work done. We get the work done on the ground level. And the kindest thing I can do for you is to tell you to get your ass on the floor. I know it's hard to write, darling. But it's harder not to. The only way you'll find out if you 'have it in you' is to get to work and see if you do. The only way to override your 'limitations, insecurities, jealousies, and ineptitude' is to produce. **"**

—*Tiny Beautiful Things*

LISTEN

In this quote Strayed identifies a feeling that many writers are familiar with. We think we should or could create an utter masterpiece, but are scared to try (lest we realize that's not true) and then end up full of self-loathing for not taking the leap. We are "up too high and down too low" in the same minute. Do you resonate with this assessment?

What do you think the "ground level" is for you personally? What is the emotional and mental space in which you can do the work?

WRITE

Strayed's advice here is blunt and to the point so this week's prompt will be as well—go "get your ass on the floor" and write!

If you need a touch more guidance than that, explore this idea of being grounded in your writing this week. What does it mean to be on the "ground floor"? What image does that evoke for you? Create a piece of writing that visually and physically captures that feeling of stability and rootedness—humble but sure—in whatever way feels most honest to you.

42

Sylvia Plath

· PERSONAL EXPERIENCE ·

" I think my poems immediately come out of the sensuous and emotional experiences I have, but I must say I cannot sympathize with these cries from the heart that are informed by nothing except a needle or a knife, or whatever it is. I believe that one should be able to control and manipulate experiences, even the most terrific, like madness, being tortured, this sort of experience, and one should be able to manipulate these experiences with an informed and an intelligent mind. I think that personal experience is very important, but certainly it shouldn't be a kind of shut-box and mirror looking, narcissistic experience. I believe it should be relevant, and relevant to the larger things, the bigger things such as Hiroshima and Dachau and so on. "

—Interview with *The Poet Speaks*

LISTEN

Plath is known and beloved for her advancement of confessional poetry, an intimately personal style of writing that focuses on the extremes of personal experience. And yet, in this quote she insists that, though personal experience is important, writing should always be "relevant to the larger things" of the world. How do you think the personal can intersect with the larger questions and issues of humanity?

Do you think that personal experience is a helpful lens through which to view large-scale issues, or do you think that the narrow perspective more often confuses the issues?

WRITE

Plath encourages us to "manipulate experiences . . . with an informed and intelligent mind." Personal experiences—whether they're your own or a character's—are most engaging to a reader when they tangle with the "larger things" of life. Since you already have an "informed and intelligent mind," you can certainly do this as well!

Begin by writing about a personal experience that feels urgent and meaningful to you. But as you write, shift your focus—how can this experience speak to a larger issue? Perhaps it reflects something about our current cultural moment, our conceptions of family, our attitude toward the environment, or our relationship with faith. How can the telling of the story, the pacing, the language, the emotion, draw readers' attention and curiosity to this more universal experience? Your aim is to write a personal story that's not really about *you* at all.

43

Gabriela Mistral

· MOTIVATION ·

" I write poetry because I can't disobey the impulse; it would be like blocking a spring that surges up in my throat. For a long time I've been the servant of the song that comes, that appears and can't be buried away. How to seal myself up now? . . . I am merely the channel. "

—Letter to Fedor Ganz (1955)

LISTEN

Mistral uses a few different kinds of language to talk about her writing experience here—it is something she "can't disobey," "a spring that surges up" within her, a song that she is merely a "servant" to, and something that can never be "buried away." Do any of those images of creativity resonate with you?

Many writers talk about their writing process in similar terms to Mistral—as if an idea grabs them by the scruff of the neck and demands to be written. On the flip side, other writers (see pg. 65 for Octavia Butler's take) speak about their process in more practical terms—as a habit, a practice, repeated choice. Writers from both camps clearly produce inspired, powerful work, but which do you resonate with more?

WRITE

Regardless of whether you're the kind of writer who approaches your work as a beautiful daily practice or tackles your projects in a fever of passion, take some inspiration from Mistral and describe your writing process. Lean into metaphor, as Mistral does, if that's helpful, or write a literal description. What does sitting down to write feel like to you—emotionally, physically, intellectually? In the moments when you've been most pleased with the work you created, how did you approach the page?

Looking over what you've written, think about how you can create a space—whether that means a physical location, time in your schedule, a steady diet of inspiration from other writers, or something else entirely—to allow your particular flavor of creativity to flourish.

44

Joyce Carol Oates

· ADMIRATION ·

❝ Most of us fall in love with works of art, many times during the course of our lifetimes. Give yourself up to admiration, even in adoration, of another's art. (How Degas worshipped Manet! How Melville loved Hawthorne! And how many young, yearning, brimming-with-emotion poets has Walt Whitman sired!) If you find an exciting, arresting, disturbing voice or vision, immerse yourself in it. You will learn from it. In my life I've fallen in love with (and never wholly fallen out of love from) writers as diverse as Lewis Carroll, Emily Brontë, Kafka, Poe. . . . **❞**

—*The Faith of a Writer*

LISTEN

Have you ever fallen in love with a work of art the way Oates describes?

As Oates acknowledges, many great artists have been strongly influenced by their love for the work of another creator. Oftentimes, we begin by imitating the work of those who we most love. Do you think imitation can be a helpful learning tool or is it more of a hindrance? (You can read up on Agatha Christie's thoughts on this on pg. 15.) What do you think the relationship is between imitation and inspiration?

WRITE

Spend some time falling head-over-heels in love with another writer. You might already have a personal favorite you'd like to revisit, or perhaps this is a time to become besotted with the writing of someone entirely new.

As you're reading, write down what you notice and love about their work. This could be as informal as some quickly jotted notes in the margins, as structured as an essay, or as whimsical as a love letter. Pay attention not only to what you love about this writer's work, but also *how* they accomplish it.

45

Ottessa Moshfegh

· LEARNING ·

" I don't really feel like I have that much agency about what I choose to do. Not that there's somebody else that has the authority, but there seems to be a karmic force in my imagination where even if I threw something away, it would just come back. Like maybe I wanna try to throw this away and *not* write this, but it would just resurrect itself in a new form. I can't really get away.

Writing projects feel a lot like if you had a guru and the guru was manipulating you so that you would have to live through certain experiences in order to learn a lesson, but the guru could have also just told you outright, 'Here's the thing you need to learn.' But you wouldn't learn it unless you spent three years suffering, you know? In a way, I know that I'm the one writing it, but I don't know if really I'm the one. I believe that there's a higher power in charge of the imagination. "

—"On Writing as a Rite of Passage"

LISTEN

Have you ever encountered an experience similar to the one Moshfegh describes here—when you feel trapped in a writing experience but have to push through and learn from it?

What is a lesson you've learned through writing through something?

WRITE

Where are you stuck right now? Are you struggling with a particular aspect of craft? With a facet of your research? With finding motivation?

Be specific and concrete about something you're struggling with—naming the problem can be half the battle. Spend this week working on it in concrete ways. Brainstorm solutions, ask for advice from others, or make yourself a mini lesson plan that lets you both learn and practice. (And hopefully working through your roadblock won't take three years of suffering like Moshfegh describes!)

46

Maggie Nelson

· WEATHER ·

" One of my good friends and mentors gave me the best advice I've ever gotten about this. He said, 'Remember, your feelings about the work don't determine the value of the work.' You can feel frustrated, disgusted, agitated, hopeless, every day, on and off, but you can't necessarily believe all your moods. You just have to keep on working.

. . .

That's a quote from Emerson, I might add. 'Our moods do not believe in each other.' Which is one of my favorite quotes because when you feel despair, despair doesn't believe in joy. And that can be very hard as a writer. If you feel like you open up your files and everything looks like shit and you're upset, that mood is going to make you want to invalidate your whole project. You just have to get kind of Buddhist about it and recognize all that is weather. **"**

—"On Working with and against Constraints"

LISTEN

Nelson shares the powerful insight that our feelings about our creative output don't necessarily reflect the quality or the content of the creative work itself. Is this something you've noticed in your own work?

On the flip side, for many creative people emotion and emotional attachment to their work is a powerful part of their process and experience. Do you find that viewing your emotions as "weather" is helpful or do they play a different role in your work?

WRITE

Over the next few days, practice writing into your moods. Whenever you sit down to write (whether that's for a luxurious few hours or a hurried few sentences, whatever it looks like for you in this season), pause before you begin and first write down where you are emotionally.

No need to write whole pages excising your feelings onto the page; a simple sentence or even a few words will do. Then dive into your project as you normally would. As you practice this habit, notice whether acknowledging your emotional state changes how you approach your writing.

Perhaps you might adjust the type of work you want to do that day based on your mood—do you find certain moods are helpful for research? Is there a frame of mind that puts you in the right place for editorial work? Be observant and curious about your own emotional weather.

47

Arundhati Roy

· FORM ·

" People always ask me about this journey from architecture to acting to screenwriting to fiction to nonfiction. And I always say that the thing is, the inquiry has always been the same. You just carry it through into different art forms. Sometimes you think, what is the most effective way of doing this? Is it a movie? Is it a building? Is it a novel? Is it an essay? "

—Interview with Nadifa Mohamed on *How to Proceed*

LISTEN

When you begin a creative project, do you consider various alternative art forms or does one leap out naturally? Have you had a project evolve as you write? (For instance you thought you were writing a short story and it turned out to be a novel. Or a section of a memoir that was really a travel essay all by itself.)

WRITE

This week experiment with changing the form of a project that you're working on. That doesn't mean throwing out your entire novel in progress and recreating it as an interpretive dance, but it could mean taking an awkward piece of dialogue you've been wrestling with and reimagining it as a prose poem, recasting a section of an essay as a fictional scene, or transforming a scene from a memoir into a screenplay.

Be thoughtful about the new form you experiment with and choose a format that captures something you want to convey in your original work. For instance, consider how a screenplay leads toward cinematic action, how an essay lends itself to contemplation and analysis, or how a haiku creates vivid imagery. Experiment and see where it leads you!

48

Jesmyn Ward

· SURPRISES ·

    ❝ When I commit to writing a story, part of what I'm really focused on, part of what I'm committed to doing when I am interested in telling a story, is to bring all the characters to life in one respect or another and make them complicated and as human as I can on the page. And so they take on shape, but . . . when I'm going back into a draft and then revising and revising, I'm still adding more dimensions. I'm still complicating them again and again and again. . . . It's a continuous task to complicate my characters and to make them more human, more believable, more, more surprising, I think. Human beings are surprising in that you never fully know, you know? You never fully know a human being. ❞

— Interview with *Minorities in Publishing*

LISTEN

Thinking through books you've loved, what have been some of the most surprising characters? Which ones have left you absolutely flabbergasted?

WRITE

We've all read endlessly about the importance of characterization and writing fully developed characters, but thinking of that process in Ward's terms—of complicating your characters "again and again and again" and making them more surprising—can be helpful.

Revisit a character and focus on doing this revisionary work. What aspects of this character can be surprising? People are never fully consistent—in their emotions, in their logic, in their thought processes—and these inconsistencies are often the exact kind of surprises that add depth and richness to a person on the page.

Consider writing a scene where your character does something completely opposite of what you might "expect." Your miserly character spends all his money on a lavish dinner, your timid wallflower takes a big leap. Now focus on framing this behavior within the character as a whole. What is the background that would make this seemingly surprising action "fit" for the character? What facet of their personality can it reveal? How can it add richness and complexity to the person you're putting on the page?

49

Joan Didion

· GRAMMAR ·

"" Grammar is a piano I play by ear, since I seem to have been out of school the year the rules were mentioned. All I know about grammar is its infinite power. To shift the structure of a sentence alters the meaning of that sentence, as definitely and inflexibly as the position of a camera alters the meaning of the object photographed. Many people know about camera angles now, but not so many know about sentences. The arrangement of the words matters, and the arrangement you want can be found in the picture in your mind. The picture dictates the arrangement. The picture dictates whether this will be a sentence with or without clauses, a sentence that ends hard or a dying-fall sentence, long or short, active or passive. The picture tells you how to arrange the words and the arrangement of the words tells you, or tells me, what's going on in the picture. *Nota bene:*

It tells you.

You don't tell it. ""

—*Let Me Tell You What I Mean*

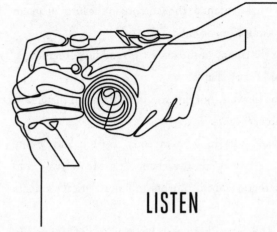

LISTEN

When you write, do you ever have a visual image, a "picture in your mind," the way Didion describes? If so, how do you connect that mental image to the grammatical choices you make?

What's your favorite quote from a book? How does the grammar used in those lines create the meaning?

WRITE

Grammar is not the sexiest of topics, but Didion makes a powerful point: the way we structure our words defines the meaning they convey. Find a sentence you've written that you love (you probably already know the one right away!) and practice altering the "position of [the] camera" by changing the grammar. Some things to consider:

- Add a visual element to the sentence in the form of an em dash, a semicolon, or italics
- Change the pacing of the sentence by adding or removing an introductory clause
- Shift the focus by burying the subject toward the end of the sentence
- Pare away everything "extraneous," Strunk and White style, or, if you're already channeling Hemingway, add some baroque embellishments and more lyrical elements

As you fiddle away, keep each iteration of the sentence in your notebook or document so you can see how it changes. Pay attention to *how* each grammatical tweak changes the meaning of the sentence itself.

50

Charlotte Brontë

· CRITICS ·

❝ The literary critic of [*the Economist*] praised the book if written by a man, and pronounced it 'odious' if the work of a woman.

To such critics I would say, 'To you I am neither man nor woman—I come before you as an author only. It is the sole ground on which you have a right to judge me—the sole ground on which I accept your judgement.' ❞

—**Letter to her editor, W. S. Williams**

LISTEN

Do you think we continue to judge a book's merit by its author's gender, race, religion, politics, etc.?

Do you think the author can and should be separated from their work, and that readers should judge a text solely based on what's on the page? Or do you think the identity of the author is a key qualification in order to write certain kinds of books or perspectives?

WRITE

Borrow the role of critic and write a piece of criticism of your own work. This isn't an invitation to let your insecurities take over (no "absolute drivel" here!) or to let your ego run free (also not "the groundbreaking masterwork of the millennium").

Instead read and review your work thoughtfully. Try to distance yourself from what you were *trying* to do and instead read simply what is on the page. What resonates? What falls flat? Be clear-eyed and honest, but also assume the best of the writer (you!) the way a good critic should.

51

Elizabeth Acevedo

· MENTORS ·

66 Look sideways. My mentors have been homies. . . . I think so often we want to look at the people who have done something already to teach us, but I found that the people who are doing alongside us are—they're studying and also trying to learn. And so, it's an incredible opportunity and an easier opportunity than to try to get a mentor or writing advisor. It's almost always easier to get a critique partner. I'll look at your works if you look at mine. And finding that trust early on, I think is critical. 99

—Interview with *Writer's Digest*

LISTEN

What role do you think trust plays in meaningful critique? Have you been part of writer's groups in the past? If so, reflect on what elements were valuable and what, if any, were a hindrance to your work.

WRITE

Take Acevedo's advice and look sideways this week! Who in your life is also working on their writing? Who can you approach about being an intentional critique partner? They might be online or in person, but reach out and see if they'd be interested!

Having a writing partner can be a powerful way to keep you motivated and help you learn, but only if you're both on the same page. A key part of a thriving writing relationship is humility—you both need to be eager and excited to learn together and from each other, instead of worrying about one-upmanship or looking the most impressive. As you look around for a writing buddy, be open about your goals and hopes and equally curious about theirs.

52

Min Jin Lee

· SILENCE AND SOUND ·

    " I am fifty years old, and after more than four decades of living in the West, I realize that like writing, talking is painful because we expose our ideas for evaluation; however, like writing, talking is powerful because our ideas may, in fact, have value and require expression.

    As a girl, I did not know this power, yet this is my power now. **"**

—**"Breaking My Own Silence"**

LISTEN

Lee highlights one of the great difficulties at the core of writing—"expos[ing] our ideas for evaluation." Does the process of writing feel vulnerable to you?

The flip side to the vulnerability is that there is, as Lee observes, great power in expression. How have you felt the power inherent in the writing process?

WRITE

Spend some time thinking about the idea or concept or question that lies at the heart of your writing. By writing you've already proven that you're brave enough to share your ideas and your voice with others (bravo!), but it can be helpful to discern what message or idea you are truly trying to express with that power.

You might know instantly the larger idea that your writing is exploring, or you might need to dig a little deeper, but try to commit it to writing in a few sentences or paragraphs. This isn't necessarily a flashy elevator pitch meant to catch the attention of others, but rather a guiding light for yourself.

Of course, there's a great deal of nuance and depth in a novel or memoir or essay that can't be contained in a single statement, but in defining the themes and concepts that are important to your work you'll be better able to weave them thoughtfully into your writing.

Bibliography

Alcott, Louisa May. Letter to Miss Churchill. December 25, 1878. https://lithub.com/louisa-may-alcotts-letter-of-advice-to-a-young-writer/.

Allende, Isabel. *The Soul of a Woman*. New York: Ballantine Books, 2021.

Atwood, Margaret. "Tell. The. Truth." In *Burning Questions*. New York: Random House US, 2022.

Austen, Jane. Letter to Cassandra Austen. February 4, 1813. *The Complete Works of Jane Austen: The Letters of Jane Austen*. East Sussex: Delphi Classics, 2017.

Baker, Jenn, and Jesmyn Ward. *Minorities in Publishing*. Episode 63. September 28, 2017. https://minoritiesinpublishing.tumblr.com/post/165830449712/episode-63-interview-with-jesmyn-ward.

Brontë, Charlotte. Letter to W. S. Williams. August 16, 1849. http://www.open.ac.uk/Arts/reading/UK/record_details.php?id=28652.

Butler, Octavia E. "Furor Scribendi." In *Bloodchild: And Other Stories*, 178–82. New York: Open Road Integrated Media, 2012.

Cheung, Alexis, and Maxine Hong Kingston. "I Can Write My Shadow." *Los Angeles Review of Books*, December 22, 2016. https://lareviewofbooks.org/article/can-write-shadow-alexis-cheung-interviews-maxine-hong-kingston/.

Christie, Agatha. *Agatha Christie: An Autobiography*. London: Harper, 2011.

Cisneros, Sandra. *The House on Mango Street*, 2nd ed. New York: Vintage Books, 2009.

Crum, Maddie, and Maggie Nelson. "On Working with and against Constraints." *The Creative Independent*, 2021. https://thecreativeinde pendent.com/people/writer-maggie-nelson-on-working-with-and -against-constraints/.

Danticat, Edwidge. *Create Dangerously: The Immigrant Artist at Work*. New York: Vintage Books, 2011.

Dickinson, Emily. Letter to Thomas Wentworth Higginson 1870. *Letters of Emily Dickinson*, vol. 1. Boston: Roberts Brothers, 1894.

Didion, Joan. *Let Me Tell You What I Mean*. New York: Knopf, 2021.

Dillard, Annie. *The Writing Life*. New York: Harper Perennial, 2013.

Eliot, George. *Silly Novels by Lady Novelists*. London: Penguin, 2010.

Ferrante, Elena. "Women Who Write." In *Frantumaglia: A Writer's Journey*. Translated by Ann Goldstein. New York: Europa Editions, 2017.

Gay, Roxane. *Writing into the Wound*. San Francisco: Scribd, 2021.

Gilbert, Elizabeth. *Big Magic*. New York: Penguin USA, 2016.

Harjo, Joy. *Poet Warrior*. New York: W.W. Norton, 2021.

Hashimi, Nadia. "On Writing Flawed, Inconsistent, Forgivable, Inspiring, and Damaged Afghan Characters." *Lit Hub*, March 22, 2021. https://lithub.com/on-writing-flawed-inconsistent-forgivable -inspiring-and-damaged-afghan-characters/.

Hurston, Zora Neale. *Dust Tracks on a Road*. New York: Harper Perennial Modern Classics, 2006.

Jemisin, N. K. "Interview: Guest Lecturer N. K. Jemisin (Part Two of

Two)." Odyssey Writing Workshop, February 2, 2016. https://
odysseyworkshop.wordpress.com/2016/02/21/interview-guest
-lecturer-n-k-jemisin-part-two-of-two/.

Jones, Amy, and Elizabeth Acevedo. "The WD Interview: Elizabeth Acevedo." *Writer's Digest*, February 18, 2022. https://www.writersdigest
.com/be-inspired/writers-digest-interview-elizabeth-acevedo.

Lahiri, Jhumpa. *In Other Words*. New York: Knopf, 2016.

Lamott, Anne. *Bird by Bird*. New York: Anchor Books, 1997.

Le Guin, Ursula K. "Where Do You Get Your Ideas From?" In *The World
Split Open*. New York: Tin House, 2014.

Lee, Min Jin. "Breaking My Own Silence." *The New York Times*, May 20,
2019. https://www.nytimes.com/2019/05/20/opinion/confidence
-public-speaking.html.

Listi, Brad, and Louise Erdrich. "Louise Erdrich." *Otherppl*. Episode 739.
November 10, 2021. https://otherpeoplepod.libsyn.com/739-louise
-erdrich.

Mistral, Gabriela. Letter to Fedor Ganz. January 4, 1955. In *Cartas*, vol.
3 of *Gabriela Mistral: Antología mayor* (Santiago: Cochrane, 1992)
574. qtd. in *Madwomen*, ed. and translated by Randall Couch. Chicago: University of Chicago Press, 2008.

Mohamed, Nadifa, and Arundhati Roy. "Aundhati Roy." *How to Proceed*.
Season 2, Episode 1. November 27, 2020. https://shows.acast.com
/how-to-proceed/episodes/arundhati-roy.

Morrison, Toni. "The Site of Memory." In *Black Ink*, 99–110. New York:
Atria, 2018.

Moss, Tyler, and Celeste Ng. "Celeste Ng: The WD Interview." *Writer's
Digest*, 2020. https://www.writersdigest.com/be-inspired/celeste
-ng-the-writers-digest-interview.

Oates, Joyce Carol. *The Faith of a Writer: Life, Craft, Art*. New York: Ecco,
2003.

O'Connor, Flannery. *Mystery and Manners: Occasional Prose*. New York:
Farrar, Straus and Giroux, 1974.

Okorafor, Nnedi. "The Sport of Writing." In *L. Ron Hubbard Presents Writers of the Future*, vol. 29. Los Angeles: Galaxy Press, 2013.

Orr, Peter, and Sylvia Plath. "A 1962 Sylvia Plath Interview with Peter Orr." *The Poet Speaks*, 1966. https://www.modernamericanpoetry .org/content/1962-sylvia-plath-interview-peter-orr.

Patchett, Ann. *These Precious Days: Essays*. New York: Harper, 2021.

Plante, David. "Jean Rhys: A Remembrance." *The Paris Review*, 76, Fall 1979.

Plimpton, George, and Maya Angelou. *Women Writers at Work*. London: The Harvill Press, 1999.

Robinson, Marilynne. "Imagination and Community." In *When I Was a Child I Read Books*. New York: Farrar, Straus and Giroux, 2012.

Salek, Yasi, and Ottessa Moshfegh. "On Writing as a Rite of Passage." *The Creative Independent*, July 16, 2018. https://thecreativeindependent .com/people/ottessa-moshfegh-on-writing-as-a-rite-of-passage/.

Smiley, Jane. "What Stories Teach Their Writers." In *Creating Fiction: Instructions and Insights from Teachers of the Associated Writing Programs*, edited by Julie Checkoway. Cincinnati: Story Press, 2004.

Smith, Jack, and Julia Alvarez. "Julia Alvarez Interview: In the Time of Discovery." *The Writer*, 2018. https://www.writermag.com/writing -inspiration/author-interviews/julia-alvarez-time-discovery/.

Smith, Zadie. "That Crafty Feeling." In *Changing My Mind: Occasional Essays*. New York: Penguin Books, 2010.

Strayed, Cheryl. *Tiny Beautiful Things: Advice on Love and Life from Dear Sugar*. New York: Random House, 2012.

Tan, Amy. *Where the Past Begins: A Writer's Memoir*. New York: Ecco, 2017.

VanZanten, Susan, and Chimamanda Ngozi Adichie. "A Conversation with Chimamanda Ngozi Adichie." *Image*, no. 65. https://image journal.org/article/conversation-chimamanda-ngozi-adichie/.

Walker, Alice. "The Unglamorous but Worthwhile Duties of the Black Revolutionary Artist, Or of the Black Writer Who Simply Works

and Writes." In *In Search of Our Mothers' Gardens: Womanist Prose.*
New York: Open Road Integrated Media, 2011.

Wharton, Edith. "Confessions of a Novelist." *The Atlantic,* April
1933. https://www.theatlantic.com/magazine/archive/1933/04
/confessions-of-a-novelist/385504/.

Wong, PP, and Han Kang. "Han Kang Interview." *Banana Writers.*
https://www.bananawriters.com/hankanginterview.

Woolf, Virginia. *The Letters of Virginia Woolf 1923–1928,* vol. 3. Edited by
Joanne Trautmann Banks and Nigel Nicolson. New York: Mariner
Books, 1980.

About the Author

VIRGINIA ANN BYRD writes from a room of her own in midcoast Maine, where she lives with her partner; a good-hearted, floppy-eared mutt; and still not enough books.